Classical

Real Repertoire

Selected and edited by Christine Brown

Contents

Faber Music 3 Queen Square London WC1N 3AU
in association with
Trinity College London 89 Albert Embankment London SE1 7TP

EDITOR'S NOTE

The pieces in *Classical Real Repertoire* have been selected to provide intermediate pianists with enjoyable music for private study or for performance in concerts, festivals and examinations. There is a wide choice as the pieces vary in technical difficulty, length, tempo, key, character and mood.

The fingering has been chosen with great care to produce good technical and musical results. The metronome marks, which are editorial, have been given as a guide but are not obligatory. The realisation of the ornaments is based on contemporary sources, frequently from the composer's own instructions. Editorial suggestions for dynamics and phrasing are shown either in brackets or, in a few places to aid clarity, by dotted lines.

The collection is not intended to be an urtext edition. As players progress they may wish to extend their knowledge of the music of this period by consulting urtext editions and making decisions for themselves. In this publication the editor has taken decisions with the intention of helping less experienced players to achieve a convincing performance in an authentic style.

I hope that these fine pieces will bring much pleasure to those who study and perform them and to their audiences.

Christine Brown

© 2005 by Faber Music Ltd and Trinity College *London*
First published in 2005 by Faber Music Ltd
in association with Trinity College *London*
3 Queen Square London WC1N 3AU
Cover design by Sue Clarke
Original handwriting by Kathy Baxendale
Music processed by Jackie Leigh
Printed in England by Caligraving Ltd

ISBN 0-571-52334-X

To buy Faber Music or Trinity publications or to find out about the full range of titles available please contact your local music retailer or Faber Music sales enquiries:

Faber Music Ltd, Burnt Mill, Elizabeth Way, Harlow CM20 2HX
Tel: +44 (0)1279 82 89 82   Fax: +44 (0)1279 82 89 83
sales@fabermusic.com   fabermusic.com   trinitycollege.co.uk

BAGATELLE IN D
Op.33 No.6

Ludwig van Beethoven
(1770–1827)

Allegretto quasi Andante [♩= *c.*66]

Con una certa espressione parlante

BAGATELLE IN E FLAT

Op.33 No.1

Ludwig van Beethoven
(1770–1827)

SCHERZANDO

from Sonatina in D, WoO 47/3

Ludwig van Beethoven
(1770–1827)

RONDO

from Sonatina in G, Op.20 No.1

Jan Ladislav Dussek
(1760–1812)

Allegretto, Tempo di Minuetto [♪ = *c.*116]

UN POCO ANDANTE

from Sonata in D, Op.25 No.6

Muzio Clementi
(1752–1832)

MENUET

from Sonata in B minor, Hob. XVI/32

Franz Joseph Haydn
(1732–1809)

The dynamics are editorial.

TRIO

Menuet da capo

ADAGIO

from Sonata in C, Hob. XVI/35

Franz Joseph Haydn
(1732–1809)

The dynamics in brackets are editorial.

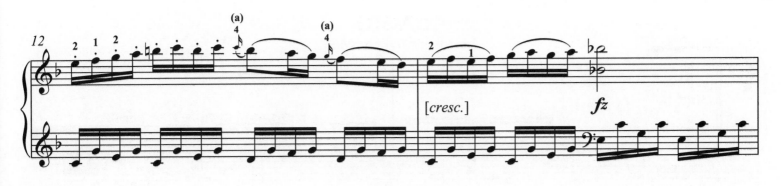

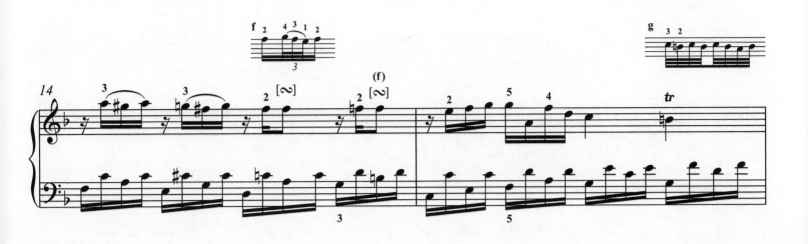

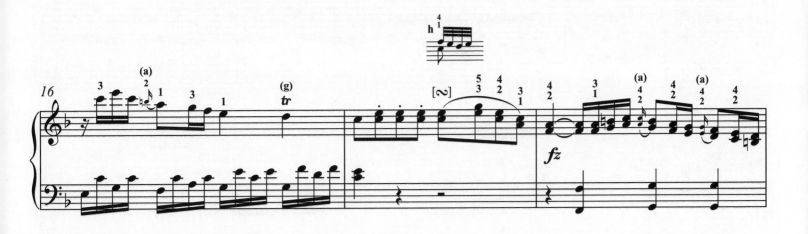

FINALE

from Sonata in D, Hob. XVI/37

Franz Joseph Haydn
(1732–1809)

The dynamics in brackets are editorial.

TO ALEXIS

Johann Nepomuk Hummel
(1778–1837)

The phrasing and fingering are from Hummel's original piano method.

ALLEGRO BURLESCO

from Sonatina in A minor, Op.88 No.3

Friedrich Kuhlau
(1786–1832)

ALLEGRO

from Viennese Sonatina in A, No.2

Wolfgang Amadeus Mozart
(1756–1791)

* Play the grace notes rapidly *on* the beat.

MINUET IN D

K.355/576b

Wolfgang Amadeus Mozart
(1756–1791)

ADAGIO

from Sonata in E flat, K.282

Wolfgang Amadeus Mozart
(1756–1791)

CODA

SCHERZO IN B FLAT

D.593/1

Franz Schubert
(1797–1828)

TRIO

Scherzo da capo

MOMENT MUSICAL IN F MINOR

Op.94 No.3 (D.780)

Franz Schubert
(1797–1828)

* Play the grace note *before* the beat.

** Play the grace notes *on* the beat and tie the A flat.

THE CLASSICAL PERIOD

The Classical period in music runs from the death of JS Bach in 1750 to about 1830. The architecture of this period moved away from the ornate Baroque style to a more restrained formality based on the style of buildings such as the Parthenon in Athens. In music there was a similar emphasis on greater clarity, order and balance, with less ornamentation. The four great composers of this period (Haydn, Mozart, Beethoven and Schubert, all of whom were connected with Vienna) led the way in developing Sonata form in instrumental music.

THE KEYBOARD INSTRUMENTS

The pieces in this collection were written for the piano, although some of them can be performed satisfactorily on earlier instruments. The piano was invented about 1700 but it did not oust the harpsichord until nearly a century later. Mozart owned both a fine two-manual harpsichord and a clavichord and it was not until 1775 that he is reported to have played the new instrument, while Haydn did not use dynamic markings suitable for the piano in his keyboard sonatas until 1777. Pedals were added to John Broadwood's instruments in 1783 and composers began to include indications for their use.

THE COMPOSERS AND THEIR PIECES

LUDWIG VAN BEETHOVEN (1770–1827) was a prodigy and at the age of thirteen, while working for the Elector of Cologne as organist and harpsichordist, he wrote his earliest piano sonatinas, dedicating them to his patron. The *Sonatina in D* was the third of this group and although the composer was still so young his personal style was already evident. Much later Beethoven wrote twenty-six pieces with the title *Bagatelle*, grouping them in three sets. Both the E flat and the D major are from the first set (1801–02). The graceful *Bagatelle in E flat* requires neat phrasing and light, even semiquavers with stronger tone in the contrasting middle section. The *Bagatelle in D* is a particularly expressive piece with an unusual marking 'Con una certa espressione parlante', meaning 'With a certain speaking expression'.

MUZIO CLEMENTI (1752–1832) was born in Italy but spent much of his life in England. He achieved fame both as a virtuoso performer and as a composer and then became well known as a teacher. He was also involved in the manufacture and development of pianos and gained a reputation as a publisher. His important set of piano studies entitled *Gradus ad Parnassum* ranges from simple five-finger exercises to advanced technique. The six *Sonatas* Op.25 were published in 1790 when Clementi was living in London. The beautiful ternary form slow movement from *Sonata No.6* is especially designed to show the singing quality of the contemporary piano.

JAN LADISLAV DUSSEK (1760–1812), a Bohemian pianist and composer, was born in a small town near Prague. He moved to Hamburg in 1782 and studied with CPE Bach. Later he settled in London where he gave many concerts, taught the piano and set up a publishing business. Haydn, who played with Dussek in London, described him as 'one of the most upright, moral, and in music, most eminent of men'. Almost all Dussek's compositions are for piano and he wrote an important treatise on piano playing.

FRANZ JOSEPH HAYDN (1732–1809) spent thirty years on the estate of the Esterhazy family composing and performing for the Prince and his guests. He wrote for the musicians available and made valuable contributions to the repertoire of string quartets, symphonies, operas and concertos. His more than fifty sonatas for the piano reveal the change in his style of writing for the contemporary keyboard instruments. The earliest ones can be performed on the harpsichord but the later ones are clearly for the piano itself as they include such indications as *crescendo*, *diminuendo* and pedal marks. The *Sonata in B major* is from his middle period and the contrast between the graceful *Minuet* in the major key and the passionate *Trio* in the minor key is very dramatic. The *Sonata in C* includes a fine slow movement in F major which is clearly for piano, not harpsichord. In the *Sonata in D major* the sonorous second movement marked 'Largo e sostenuto' (a marking clearly unsuitable for the earlier instruments) is followed by a delightful *Finale* which has become popular for its tuneful character.

JOHANN NEPOMUK HUMMEL (1778–1837), the Austrian composer and pianist, was a child prodigy and a pupil of Mozart. His technique was so amazingly good that at concerts audiences would even stand to watch his hands. He wrote a comprehensive piano tutor entitled *Klavierschule* which was published in both Austrian and English editions and included the expressive piece dedicated *To Alexis*.

FRIEDRICH KUHLAU (1786–1832) was born in Germany and studied with a pupil of CPE Bach, but he spent most of his life in Denmark where he was appointed a court chamber musician and became famous as a pianist and composer. Written for his pupils, his *Sonatinas* for piano have remained popular to this day as learning to play them well fosters the development of a good piano technique.

WOLFGANG AMADEUS MOZART (1756–1791) was improvising minuets at the keyboard at the age of five, but the *Minuet in D*, dating from about 1789, is a mature work with beautiful chromatic writing similar to that found in the *Adagio in B minor* and the *Rondo in A minor*, which were written in the same period. The suggested speed will allow the performer time to express the pathos of the harmonies and the poetry of the graceful contrapuntal writing. It was in Vienna, where he chose to settle, that Mozart wrote the six *Viennese Sonatinas*. They are less demanding both technically and musically than his sonatas and provide an ideal introduction to his style. The mature *Sonata in E flat* is unusual in that it opens with a slow movement which expresses deep emotion and highlights the character of the emerging piano.

FRANZ SCHUBERT (1797–1828) was not a concert pianist but he played the piano all his life and wrote an amazingly large quantity of music for the instrument, including large scale sonatas, small scale dances, two sets of impromptus and the six *Moments Musicaux* (1823–28). The smaller pieces were not intended for performance at public concerts, but for domestic musical evenings known as Schubertiads, when a circle of musical friends gathered to sing and play for one another. The *Moment Musical in F minor*, perhaps the most well known of Schubert's small piano works, has the character of a dance and is memorable for its gentle ending in the tonic major. The *Scherzo in B flat* is an early work, finely structured and showing an appreciation of the varied tonal colours of the early piano by using a lower pitch for the *Trio*.